Hello,
my name is Sparky
and I am a great inventor.
Clever, right? Welcome! I am
here to give you ideas on how to build
your skills with NSW Foundation
Style cursive handwriting.

## My inventor's profile

Name: _____

Class: _____        Birthday: _____

Place of birth: _____

Two interesting facts about me:

1. _____

2. _____

Three things I'd like to invent:

1. _____

2. _____

3. _____

# My progress passport

Inventors and innovators come from all over the world! Some of the most important inventions came from Africa and Asia (such as pottery, the wheel, glass and paper), but they were so long ago that we don't know the names of the individual inventors. This is equally true of the First Nations Australians who invented many items and continue to develop practices that show both resourcefulness and a great knowledge of science.

As you work through this book, write the name of the person next to their invention, discovery or contribution.

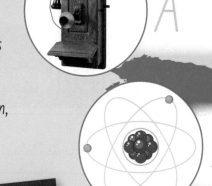

A

J

Look for this icon to find the right name.

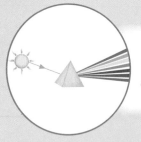

R

I

R

OXFORD UNIVERSITY PRE

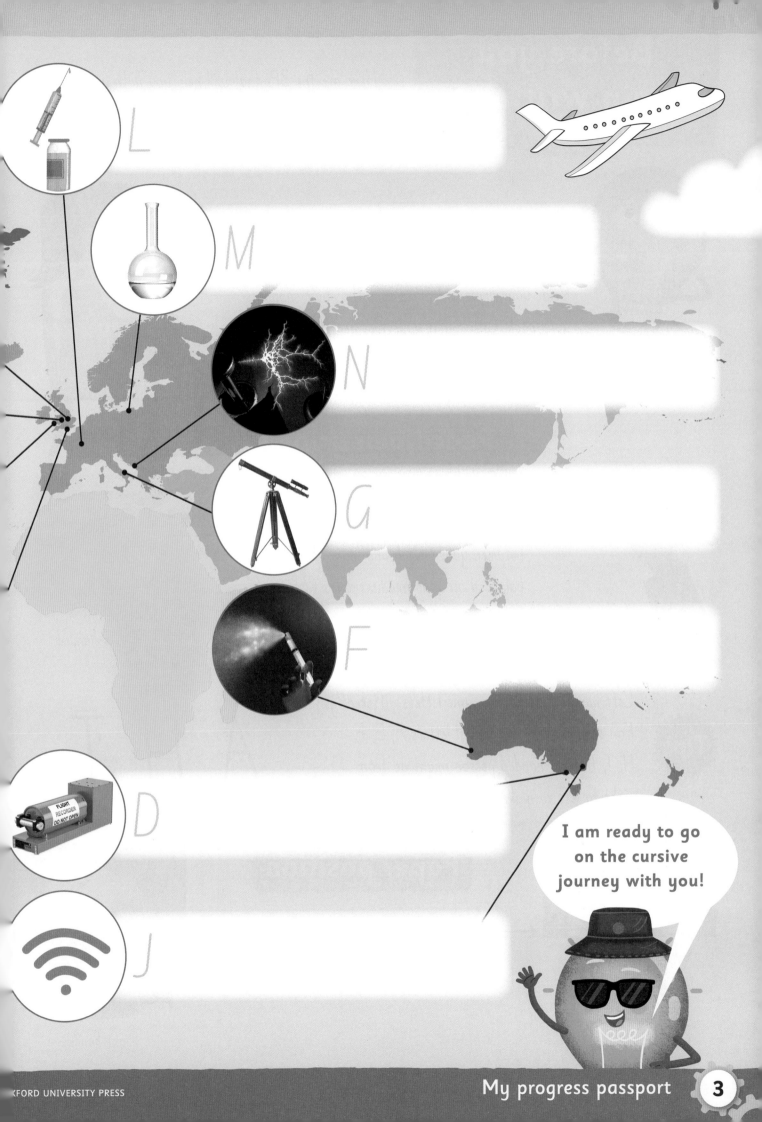

# Before you begin writing ...

Here are the **3Ps** that will help you with your writing: **p**osture, **p**encil/pen grip and **p**aper position. You will be reminded about these as you work through the book.

## Posture

Relax your arms and make sure the chair supports your back. Check that your feet are flat on the floor.

## Pencil/pen grip

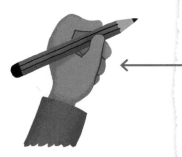

Left-handed

How you hold your pencil/pen is most important. Hold your pencil/pen firmly between your thumb and index finger, balanced on your middle fingers (2.5 cm before the end and not too tightly!).

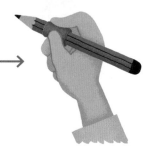

Right-handed

Tip!

Left-handers may form some letters differently. For example, for the capital letters A, E, F, H, T, the left-handed person might go from right to left to make the join:

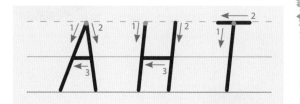

## Paper position

Left-handed

Angle your page and use your non-writing hand to steady the page.

Right-handed

# Revision

## Foundation Style print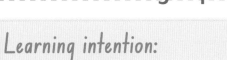

**Learning intention:**
To revise NSW Foundation Style print handwriting

> Before we begin on our adventure to meet all the famous inventors around the world, let's revise our print handwriting.

Trace these letters, punctuation marks and numbers.

aA  bB  cC  dD  eE  fF  gG  hH

iI  jJ  kK  lL  mM  nN  oO  pP

qQ  rR  sS  tT  uU  vV  wW  xX

yY  zZ  "  "  ,  ?  !  .

0  1  2  3  4  5  6  7  8  9  10

Copy the names of these countries. Link the capital letter to the matching lower-case letter or letters in that word, for example, Australia.

Australia    Albania    Barbados    Georgia

Eritrea    India    Timor-Leste    Uruguay

## Exits and entries

**Learning intention:**
To revise letters that contain exit and entry flicks

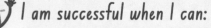

I am successful when I can:
- ☐ check my 3Ps
- ☐ make my entry and exit flicks smooth rather than pointy.

Trace the alphabet with all its entries and exits.

a b c d e f g h i j k l m

n o p q r s t u v w x y z

Copy the text below.

Throughout my book I will be

practising my cursive handwriting,

using many entries, exits and joins.

I am going to try my best!

**Self-assessment**

- Draw a star on top of your neatest three exit flicks.
- Draw a heart on top of your neatest three entry flicks.

# Diagonal joins

**Tip!**

We know a diagonal join goes from one letter's exit flick up to meet the next letter. Practise the diagonal joins below. Remember, the pencil/pen stays on the paper.

*an*

Trace and then copy these diagonal joins.

ai    am    an    ap    ar    au    ay

e    cu    cy    de    di    du    dy

n    em    ei    ey    he    hi    hu

Copy this sentence to practise your diagonal joins.

Creativity and effort shape the world.

# Diagonal joins to tall letters

this ✓    not this ✗

crossbar →

*at*    *at*

**Tip!** Remember to add the crossbar last.

Trace and then copy these diagonal joins.

*at*    *at*    *at*    *at*    *at*    *at*    *at*

*it*    *it*    *it*    *it*    *it*    *it*    *it*

*ut*    *ut*    *ut*    *ut*    *et*    *et*    *et*    *et*

Copy this sentence to practise your diagonal joins.

*Put on your inventor's hat, use*

*your imagination and make history*

# Drop-in joins

**Tip!** When we join to anti-clockwise letters (such as a, c, d, g and q), the exit from the first letter reaches high towards the top of the anti-clockwise letter. Take the exit flick up high!

The a touches the exit here.

*na*

Trace and then copy these drop-in joins for a, c, d, g and q.

la    ia    ha    ac    ec    uc    ed    id    ld

ag    ma    ig    aq    eq    ng    ca    ud    nq

Trace and then copy these words, which include letters with drop-in joins.

Alexander Graham Bell invented the telephone

in 1876. Two cans linked by a string will

show you how.

Passport

# Horizontal joins

**Tip!** The horizontal join for o, r, u, w and x has a slight dip. The horizontal join from f goes straight across.

slight dip

*on  ri  vu  wi  xi  fi*

Trace and then copy these horizontal joins.

oi   om   on   op   or   ou   ov   oy

ri   rm   rn   rp   rr   ru   rv   ry

vi   vu   vv   vy   ti   vu   vv   vy

wi   wm   wn   wr   wy   wi   wr

xi   xi   xp   xp   xu   xu   xy   fi

# Horizontal joins to anti-clockwise letters

Learning intention:
To write anti-clockwise letters
with horizontal joins

**Tip!** When writing horizontal joins to anti-clockwise letters, go across to the start of the letter, then **retrace**.

*oa fc*

Trace and then copy these letter pairs and words.

*oa    oc    oo    og    os    od    oa    oc    oo*

*ra    rc    ro    rg    rs    rd    xa    xc    xo*

*va    vc    vo    fa    fo    fc    va    vo*

*vacuum    waves    vibrations    radio*

*locomotive phonograph aeroplane forward*

# Horizontal joins to tall letters

I am successful when I can:
- [ ] check my 3Ps
- [ ] write horizontal joins to tall letters.

**Tip!** When you make a join to tall letters, go right to the top and then retrace a little as you move downwards.

rk

Trace and then copy these letter pairs.

ol     ob     oh     ol     ok     of

rt     rk     rt     rb     rh     rt     rf

wk     wh     wl     wt     xl     xt     xf     xh

**Self-assessment**

Assess your horizontal joins.

   [ ] I need some more practice

   [ ] I'm making progress

   [ ] I've got it!

**Teacher comment**

# Letters that do not join

**Learning intention:**
To write letters that have clockwise finishers

 **Tip!** Letters that finish in a clockwise direction do not join.

b g j p s y

Trace and then copy these letters that finish in a clockwise direction.

b g j p s y

Copy these letter pairs and words on the lines below.

ba    baby    be    bean    ga    gave

go    goal    ji    jigsaw    jo    joke

pa    paper    po    pot    sa    sails

si    sight    ye    yes    yo    young

# Capital letters

**Tip!** Remember that capital letters do not join.

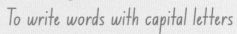

Trace and then copy these capital letters.

A  B  C  D  E  F  G

- - - - - - - - - - - - - - - - - -

H  I  J  K  L  M  N

- - - - - - - - - - - - - - - - - -

O  P  Q  R  S  T  U

- - - - - - - - - - - - - - - - - -

V  W  X  Y  Z

- - - - - - - - - - - - - - - - - -

Copy these place names.

Sydney     New South Wales     Australia

- - - - - - - - - - - - - - - - - -

Copy the sentence below, which includes letters that do and do not join.

James Chadwick was an English physicist.

He proved the existence of neutrons, for

which he received the Nobel

Prize in Physics in 1935.

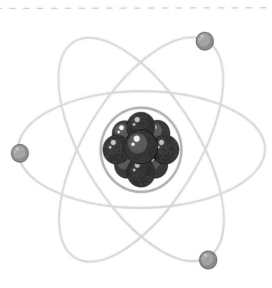

**Teacher comment**

Passport

# Joins from q to u

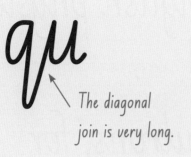

qu

↖ The diagonal
join is very long.

Trace and then copy these letter pairs with qu joins.

qu    qu    qu    qu    qu    qu    qu

Copy these words and then draw a line to match each word to its picture. The first one is done for you.

queen    quilt    question    quiet    quick    quokka

queen

# Fluency patterns

**Tip!** Take your time here to practise your fluency joins. Getting this right will help you throughout your cursive handwriting journey.

Copy these fluency patterns.

# Consolidating

**Tip!** Remember to always use printing for the labels on maps and diagrams.

Label the diagram with the words at the bottom of the page. Use print handwriting. One is done for you.

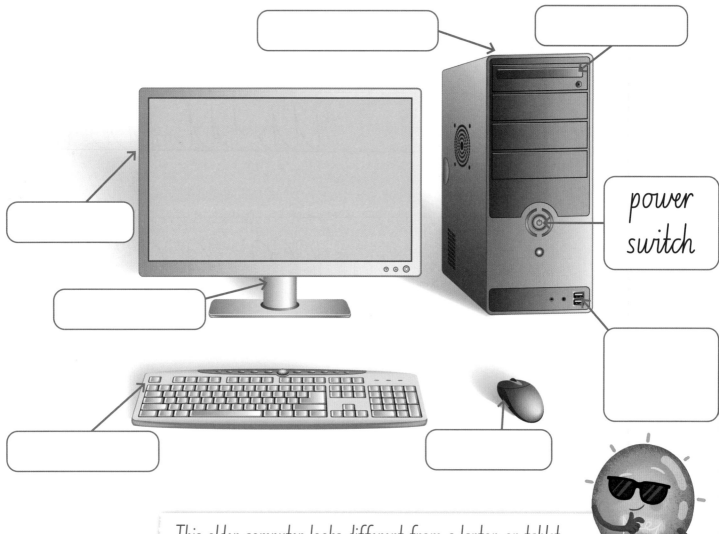

power switch

This older computer looks different from a laptop or tablet, but you can see how they have some of the same features.

| monitor | hard drive | keyboard | mouse |
|---|---|---|---|
| ~~power switch~~ | stand | CD drive | USB port |

# Assessment: All joins

With a coloured pencil, shade the letter pairs that would have a diagonal join.

| | | | | |
|---|---|---|---|---|
| mp | Fa | al | xy | fi |
| ac | If | Lm | ox | of |
| be | ng | cr | Ja | oh |
| hi | or | de | po | rk |

*The a touches the exit here.*    *slight dip*

**an**    **na**    **on**

diagonal join    drop-in join    horizontal join

With a coloured pencil, shade the letter pairs that would have a horizontal join.

| | | | | |
|---|---|---|---|---|
| mp | Fa | al | xy | fi |
| ac | If | Lm | ox | of |
| be | ng | cr | Ja | oh |
| hi | or | de | po | rk |

With a coloured pencil, shade the letter pairs that would have a drop-in join.

| | | | | |
|---|---|---|---|---|
| mp | Fa | al | xy | fi |
| ac | If | Lm | ox | of |
| be | ng | cr | Ja | oh |
| hi | or | de | po | rk |

**Self-assessment**

Assess how you are going with all joins.

 ❑ I need some more practice

 ❑ I'm making progress

 ❑ I've got it!

**Teacher comment**

# Tricky joins

## Joins to s

Learning intention:
To join our letters to the letter s

rs retrace

rs retrace

**Tip!** We use horizontal joins to connect letters to s.

This requires some retracing at the top of the finishing letters.

Go across to form the top of the s, then retrace the top on your way down.

Trace these horizontal joins to s. Then use a coloured pencil to colour where you retraced the letter s.

| os | rs | vs | ws | xs | fs |
|----|----|----|----|----|-----|
| os | rs | vs | ws | xs | fs |

Trace and then copy these words.

loss    first    flowers    position    chefs    claws

screws    closer    verse    swimmers    boost

S can also be joined to other letters by using a diagonal join.

**as** retrace

**as** retrace

Trace these diagonal joins to s. Then, using another colour pencil, colour the diagonal join and retrace.

as   cs   ds   es   hs   is   ks   ls   ms   ns   ts

Trace and then copy these words.

hands   best   last   this   cakes   music

sunset   cracks   bells   fishing   tracks

fashion   physics   invents   seams   myths

# Joins to e

smooth diagonal join

ne

horizontal dip join

re

**Tip!** Diagonal joins to e are a smooth upward stroke. Horizontal joins to e have a bigger dip than usual.

Trace and then copy this pattern.

eeleeleel

Trace and then copy these horizontal joins to e in the space on the same line.

oe    re    ve    we    xe

Trace and then copy these words.

poems    whichever    save    taxes    core    believe

travel    before    stare    weather    canoe

# Joins to f

**Learning intention:** To drop our f's into place

**Tip!** When writing diagonal joins to f, the f is dropped in.

Use a diagonal join to practise these joins to f.

*af    ef    if    uf    lf    af    ef    if    uf    lf*

*calf    sniff    before    raffle    yourself    puff*

*life    reef    strife*

*unify    whiff    afloat*

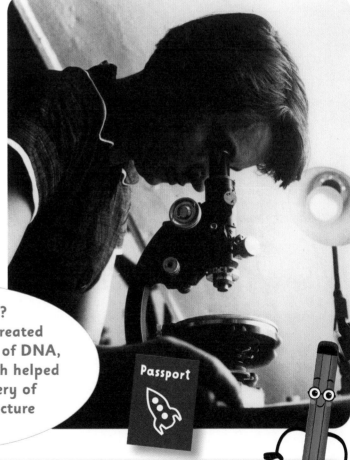

**Did you know?**
Rosalind Franklin created the first X-ray picture of DNA, called Photo 51, which helped lead to the discovery of the molecular structure of DNA.

**Self-assessment**    Draw a star on your neatest three joins to f. ⭐

For horizontal joins to f, part of the f is retraced.
Use a horizontal join to practise these joins to f.

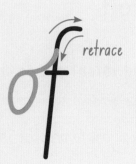
retrace

I am successful when I can:
❑ add a horizontal join to f
❑ retrace part of the f.

of rf uf xf of rf uf xf of rf uf xf

coffee   sofa   colourful   lawful   boxful

scarf   lift-off   surf   Oxford   snowfall

Copy this sentence.

Ms Orfanos fished for

five hours at the beach.

OXFORD UNIVERSITY PRESS

# More f joins

**Learning intention:**
To drop our f's into place

**Tip!** When f joins to t, you can use one longer crossbar. This is done in three steps. Do the crossbar last.

Trace and then copy these letter pairs to practise your joins from f to t.

ft     ft     ft     ft     ft

Trace and then copy these words with joins from f to t.

craft     after     left     shift     often

softly     fifty     swift     lift     loft     heft

Trace and then copy these words with joins to and from the letter f.

waterfall     different     follow     forest     after

lift     fiftieth     fishing     fixed     magnify

Copy these sentences.

Did you know that the technology to create

wireless networks was invented in Australia?

In 1992, Dr John O'Sullivan and the

CSIRO developed technology to reduce the

echo of radio waves, which allows wifi to

work. It is now used by billions of people

and has changed the way we live.

OXFORD UNIVERSITY PRESS

# Consolidating

**Learning intention:**

To review all I have learnt with cursive handwriting

Copy these sentences.

Cameras from years ago were often heavy,

bulky and awkward to handle. They were

very sensitive to changes in light levels, and

any shaking would make the photo look

blurred. These days, cameras are small,

portable and have many features.

# Assessment: Tricky joins

Copy this selection of inventions. With a coloured pencil, go over any drop-in, horizontal or diagonal joins.

*telephone  typewriter  handwriting  compass*

*fruit peeler  sponge  battery  kettle  computer*

*nail  sewing machine  alarm clock  black box*

Complete the sentence below.

*My favourite invention is _____*

*because _____.*

**Self-assessment**

Assess how you are going with tricky joins.

 ❏ I need some more practice

 ❏ I'm making progress

 ❏ I've got it!

**Teacher comment**

OXFORD UNIVERSITY PRESS

# Smaller lines

## Writing on smaller lines

Did you know that if you could travel as fast as light, the universe would look very different?

Well, I don't expect you to travel at the speed of light, but writing on smaller lines will help you write faster!

Copy these sentences to practise writing on smaller lines.

To help make your writing a little faster, we will practise

writing on smaller lines. Make sure you have checked your

3Ps and then copy these sentences in your neatest handwriting.

Check that you have joined letters correctly. Remember that

capital letters and the letters b, g, j, p, s and y don't join.

**Self-assessment**　　Circle your neatest three words!

# More tricky joins

## Practising tricky joins

Copy the sentences below to practise your tricky joins.

An Italian astronomer and mathematician, Galileo Galilei

is known as the father of modern astronomy and physics.

He lived from 1564 to 1642. His improvements to the telescope

led to key astronomical discoveries, including that the Earth

revolves around the Sun.

Albert Einstein credited Galileo

as being more responsible for

the birth of modern science than

any other person.

# Joins from f to l

**Learning intention:**
To use the crossbar to join f to l

We use the crossbar to join from f to l, then retrace on the way down.

Trace and then copy these letter pairs to practise your joins from f to l.

fl    fl    fl    fl    fl    fl

Copy these sentences.

Darri saw some flying fish flip, flop, flap and float in the air.

She wondered if these fish had inspired Leonardo da Vinci to

envisage a flying machine, which he did many drawings of.

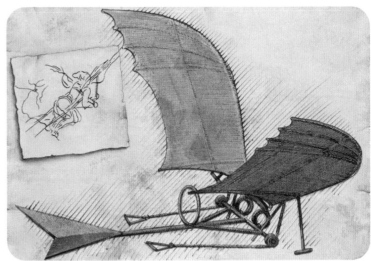

# Letters with no exits

## o  v  w

Copy these words.

cow      snow      Liv      lotto      grow      two

window      potato      also      buffalo      Gustav

**Fine motor skills task:** Colour in this picture. Add a caption, using words from the list above.

# Double letters

**Tip!** Make sure your double letters are not too far apart. Remember that the single crossbar does all the joining for double f.

Trace and then copy these letter pairs.

*dd*　　*ee*　　*ff*　　*gg*　　*ll*　　*mm*　　*nn*　　*oo*

*pp*　　*rr*　　*tt*　　*zz*　　*oo*　　*bb*　　*cc*　　*ss*

Copy these words with double letters.

address　　keen　　wiggle　　terrestrial　　sunny　　pool

cliff　　app　　worry　　bedazzle　　valley

broccoli　　fluff　　poppy　　bubble　　watt

withhold　　messy　　hiccup　　savvy　　bookkeeper

# Joins to the shorter s

Today you are going to learn a new way to join to the letter s.

**✗ OLD**   **✓ NEW**

$es \longrightarrow es$

Did you notice the top of the s is now shorter? There is less to retrace, which will make your writing faster!

Trace and then copy these letter pairs to practise diagonal joins to the shorter s.

*es    es    es    es    es    es    es    es    es*

Trace and then copy these letter pairs to practise horizontal joins to the shorter s.

*rs    rs    rs    rs    rs    rs    rs    rs    rs*

Trace and then copy these letter pairs.

*as    cs    ds    es    hs    is    ks    ls    ms    ns    us*

*atoms    beams    optics    myths    aeons    gadgets*

*os    rs    vs    ws    os    rs    vs    ws    os    rs    vs*

*cars    mirrors    videos    wheelbarrows    scissors    screws*

Trace and then copy these words.

On 16 July 1969, NASA launched the spacecraft Apollo 11 into

space from NASA's Kennedy Space Center. Four days later,

millions of people watched astronauts Neil Armstrong and

Edwin "Buzz" Aldrin walk on the Moon. The third astronaut,

Michael Collins, did not land on the

Moon. However, the mission would

not have been possible without his

skills as a command module pilot.

# Consolidating

Copy the following text to practise your cursive handwriting.

Sir Isaac Newton was a famous scientist and mathematician.

He explained gravity and developed the theory of colour.

Newton's experiments of light and colour have contributed

greatly to our world today. His "crucial experiment" proved that

light is made up of different colours, rather than light being

coloured by a prism.

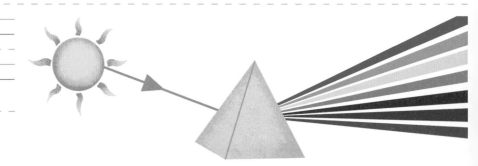

**Self-assessment**

Assess your print to cursive handwriting.

 ❏ I need some more practice

 ❏ I'm making progress

 ❏ I've got it!

**Teacher comment**

**Passport**

# Assessment: More tricky joins

Copy the fl words below.

flew        flag        flint        flame        flask        flimsy

Copy the qu words below.

quick        quiver        quarter        quack        quiet

Remember that the letters o, v and w have no exits if they appear at the end of a word. Copy the words below.

potato        Viv        radio        volcano        arrow        grow

Copy these words with double letters.

wiggle        constellation        stellar        fluff        valley

mission        satellite        wobble        mass        parallel

**Teacher comment**

# Handwriting hints

## Letter size and spacing

I am successful when I can:
- ☐ check my 3Ps
- ☐ write faster using smaller lines.

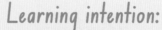

**Tip!** Watch your horizontal joins don't go too far before connecting to the next letter.

Focus on your letter size and spacing as you copy these sentences.

Marie Curie was a Polish-French physicist and chemist who

discovered polonium and radium, and conducted research on

radioactivity. She was the first woman to win a Nobel prize

and the first person to win two Nobel prizes in different sciences.

When World War I broke out in Europe, Curie realised that

X-rays could help doctors to work out what was wrong with

injured soldiers. Curie and her daughter Irène set up 200

radiology units during the first two years of the war, which

helped to save many lives. Her research also led to the use

of radiation to treat cancer. The legacy of Curie's work has

contributed to shaping life in the 21st century. Marie Curie is

one of the most famous scientists in history.

**Self-assessment**   Assess how you are going with letter size and spacing.

❑ I need some more practice

❑ I'm making progress

❑ I've got it!

**Teacher comment**

Passport

# Spacing between letters

**Learning intention:**

To focus on the size and spacing between letters

**I am successful when I can:**
- ❑ check my 3Ps
- ❑ write faster on smaller lines.

# computer

**Tip!**

**Kerning:** *(noun)* The spacing between letters in a word.

All letters in words should be as evenly spaced as possible. This makes your writing neater and easier to read.

Rewrite the word "computer" with even letter spacing on the lines below.

com pu te r

uneven spacing

computer

not enough spacing

computer

correct spacing

These letter pairs do not have the correct spacing. Rewrite them with the correct spacing.

ai    ld    hi    ck    le    tt    ay

wh    ed    ry    op    oo    nd    th

**Teacher comment**

# Spacing between words

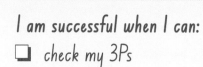

I am successful when I can:
- ☐ check my 3Ps
- ☐ make spaces even
- ☐ write letters of the same size.

**Learning intention:**

To focus on the size and spacing between words

**Tip!** Looking at these sound waves, you can see spaces. There is also a space bar on the keyboard. We need spaces in sound, in our typing and in our writing to make sense of things.

Rewrite this passage, using even spaces between the words.

When words are   too close together or too

far apart, it makes the writing   difficult to

read.  The spaces between  words need to be even, and letters must

be of the same size. When words   are spaced evenly   and letters

are of  the same size,   the writing is   much easier   to read.

**Self-assessment**

Assess how you are going with the size and spacing between words.

- ☐ I need some more practice
- ☐ I'm making progress

- ☐ I've got it!

**Teacher comment**

Copy this passage, keeping a consistent size for your letters and even spaces between the words.

Professor Fiona Wood is a British-born Australian plastic

surgeon and burns specialist who lives in Perth. Professor Wood

and her co-inventor, Marie Stoner, invented "spray-on skin" to

help people with burns. This technique was a world first and has

saved the lives of thousands of people who have suffered severe

burns. In 2005 Fiona Wood

was named Australian of the Year.

Copy these words to practise correct size and spacing.

holidays     golf     jet     Peter     computer     collaborate

telephone     quietly     Frankie     inventor     surgery

# Slope

Learning intention: To write using a slope

**Tip!** Use the slope card at the back of your book to help you. Place it behind the page you are writing on to help keep the slope of your writing consistent.

x Sparky

✓ Sparky

Trace and then copy these fluency patterns with the slope card.

Copy these words, keeping a consistent slope.

slope     handwriting     cursive     angle     direction

mountain     crater     tilt     orbit     eclipse

typewriter     bicycle     stapler     lawnmower     chess

# Consolidating

Survey ten people in your class. Ask them which one of these inventions they would not want to give up. Use tally marks to collect your data.

| Computer | Washing machine | Electric toothbrush | Video-game console |
|---|---|---|---|
|  | | | |
| | | | |

Present your information in a column graph below. Remember to label your graph.

In cursive handwriting, write two comments about the information you have gathered, such as the most or least popular invention.

1.

2.

OXFORD UNIVERSITY PRES

*Copy these sentences, focusing on the spacing, size and slope.*

Rachel Carson was an American marine

biologist, nature writer and conservationist.

In 1962 she wrote an influential book called

"Silent Spring", which exposed the harmful effects of pesticides

on the environment. She is credited with advancing the global

environmental movement. She once said, "One way to open your

eyes is to ask yourself, 'What if I had never seen this before?'"

Passport

# Assessment: Handwriting hints

Rewrite the following sentences in cursive handwriting, using the correct spacing, size and slope.

Have you ever daydreamed about something you'd like

to build? How would you get started? Would you create

marvellous machines, groovy gadgets, winner wheels or

awesome aircraft?

Everyone is capable of inventing or discovering things.

Wilbur and Orville Wright (the Wright Brothers) were

among the first to build and fly an aeroplane with an engine.

**Self-assessment**

 Assess how you are going with spacing, size and slope.

 ❏ I need some more practice

 ❏ I'm making progress

 ❏ I've got it!

**Teacher comment**

# Fluency and legibility

## Letters and words

Wow! I'm impressed with your hole in one!

Copy the letters and sentences below to practise your fluency.

abcdefghijklmnopqrstuvwxyz

Peter practised golf every day for weeks. He took golf lessons and

practised his putting, chipping and driving to improve his golf

and lower his handicap score. What a great sport!

# Common blends and digraphs

Trace these common blends (letter combinations in which each letter makes a sound) and words. Copy them on the lines below and then add two more words of your own for each letter combination.

gr     great     green

pl     plan     please

nd     bland     grand

bl     blue     black

nk     blank     thank

spr     spring     sprung

squ     squash     squid

tr      tree      trunk

ck      brick      crack

ft      soft      left

br      bridge      break

ll      bell      fell

thr      three      through

scr      scrape      screen

First Nations Australians cut bark from trees, without damaging the tree, to create watertight canoes.

Trace and then copy these letter combinations and words. Remember to use the correct joins. Then add two more words of your own for each digraph. (A digraph is two letters that make one sound.)

oa     throat     float

ea     leaf     deaf

ch     reach     beach

th     throw     think

gh     laugh     cough

sh     ship     sharp

oo     pool     didgeridoo

ee     sheep     need

ie     chief     brief

ei     receive     ceiling

Rewrite these words, including the prefix. For example, un- + happy = unhappy. The first one is done for you.

| un- | happy | tidy | do | tie | likely |
|-----|-------|------|-----|-----|--------|

unhappy

| dis- | appear | like | able | trust |
|------|--------|------|------|-------|

| re- | arrange | appear | draw | write |
|-----|---------|--------|------|-------|

| tri- | angle | cycle | athlete | pod |
|------|-------|-------|---------|-----|

| mis- | place | use | lead | understand |
|------|-------|-----|------|------------|

nvented by First Nations Australians, the didgeridoo
s a wind instrument made from hollowed-out trees
r branches.

**Common blends and digraphs**

# High-frequency words

Copy the two words on each line twice and then use both in a short sentence on the line below. The first one is done for you.

Learning intention:
To write high-frequency words in cursive handwriting

 **Tip!** Remember that your sentences need to make sense. Try saying them out loud to check.

friends    *friends    friends*    because    *because    because*

*I like my friends because they make me smile.*

next                              school

girl                              stopped

queen                             window

fish                              jumped

animals                           sun

floppy                            tree

green                             garden

| | |
|---|---|
| everyone | shouted |
| another | way |
| dark | suddenly |
| better | town |
| think | king |
| wish | different |
| keep | key |
| water | fun |

Circle your three neatest words in cursive handwriting.

High-frequency words

# Revision

Copy the text below to practise your spacing, size and slope.

Nikola Tesla was a Serbian-American scientist and inventor

who specialised in working with electricity. He took after his

mother, who was a scientist and had an enormous passion

for science. Tesla worked with Thomas Edison until they had

a major disagreement on the type of electricity to use for new

inventions. This led Tesla to found his own company, the

Tesla Electric Light Company.

Copy these inventions.

remote control

alternating current (AC) electricity

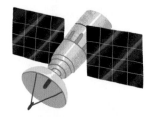

satellite radar

*Copy these sentences.*

An Australian named David Warren invented the black

box flight recorder in 1954. These black box flight recorders

(which are actually orange) let air-crash investigators listen

to conversations and retrieve flight data that were recorded

before the crash. This helps to work out the cause of a crash,

which can help prevent future accidents. At first, there was

a lack of interest in this invention in Australia. However, in

1967, Australia became the first country to make the black box

mandatory in major aircraft.

# Consolidating

Copy the words below. Then, using the words and your own ideas, create an advertisement on the billboard below to sell a new phone. Be sure to present your advertisement neatly.

sale     best price     music     volume

apps     technology     photos     charger

invention     camera     features     warranty

# Assessment: Fluency and legibility

Rewrite these sentences in cursive handwriting. Assess your handwriting at the bottom of the page.

So far, throughout this book, you have become familiar with

different inventors who have come from all around the

world. You have met inventors from the United Kingdom,

the United States of America, Poland, Italy, France, Serbia

and Australia. They have all had a major influence and

impact on our world today.

Test your memory. On a separate piece of paper, list as many of the inventors you've read about in this book as you can. Then check to see if you've missed any. Remember to go back and fill in your passport.

**Self-assessment**

Assess the fluency and legibility of your handwriting.

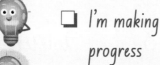

☐ I need some more practice

☐ I'm making progress

☐ I've got it!

**Teacher comment**

## Punctuation marks

Learning intention:
To write and revise punctuation marks

Edit the text below by filling in the missing letters and the correct punctuation. The words in bold are defined in the glossary that follows the text.

Louis Pasteur was born on 20 December 1822 _e was born in Dole, France _asteur was skilled in drawing and painting gaining a Bachelor of Arts degree in 1840 _his talented man was also interested in science and later gained a Bachelor of Science degree _asteur was one of the most famous **microbiologists** in history _id you know that his findings changed the world of medicine forever _asteur studied researched and then invented a whole new process where bacteria could be removed by boiling water _his became known as **pasteurisation** _n 1879 _asteur invented the first vaccine _hrough _asteur's discovery of **vaccines** thousands of people have survived fatal illnesses _n incredible innovator microbiologist  artist and scientist   _ouis _asteur died on 28 September 1895 at the age of 72_ _asteur once said,  Science knows no country, because knowledge belongs to humanity. _is legacy changed the world

Glossary

**microbiologist:** an expert in microorganisms

**pasteurisation:** sterilisation of a product to make it safe to consume

**vaccine:** a substance used to produce antibodies to fight disease

I am successful when I have included:

- ❏ 16 capital letters
- ❏ 10 full stops
- ❏ 8 commas
- ❏ 1 question mark
- ❏ 1 set of speech marks
- ❏ 1 exclamation mark.

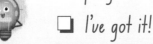

# Numerals

Learning intention:

To write numerals legibly

182

Copy these number words and then write them as numerals. The first one is done for you.

ninety-two                          twelve

*ninety-two 92*

eighty-five                         fourteen

fifty-eight                         five hundred

thirty-two thousand                 seventy-three

Write these numerals as words.

99

14

296

408

840

1500

OXFORD UNIVERSITY PRES

Complete these number patterns.

5 10 15 20 _ _ _ _ _

3 5 7 9 _ _ _ _ _ _

44 55 66 77 _ _ _ _ _ _

100 150 200 250 _ _ _ _ _

Complete the fact file about a famous inventor in this book, or you can write about another inventor that you know about.

Inventor's name:

Date of birth: __ / __ / ____

Country of birth:

Invention or discovery:

Description of invention or discovery:

# Timeline

Match the invention to the correct year on the timeline, and then complete the answer on the line provided.

You will know the answers from reading this book. (You can see the page reference in brackets at the end of each information box.)

The CSIRO and _____ developed technology to reduce the echo of radio waves, which allowed wifi to work. (See page 26.)

Write the name of one of the astronauts on Apollo 11, which made the first crewed landing on the Moon. (See page 35.)

This invention is used to help find out what happened when a plane crashes. (See page 55.)

This Australian of the Year specialises in burns treatments. (See page 42.)

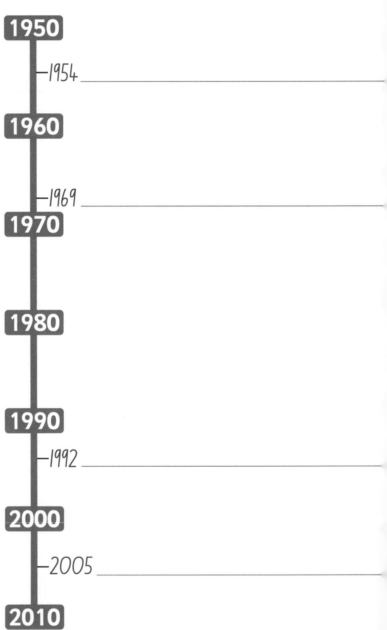

1950

—1954 _____

1960

—1969 _____

1970

1980

1990

—1992 _____

2000

—2005 _____

2010

# Crossword

The number in brackets following the clue is the number of letters in each word. Your teacher can see the completed crossword in the Teacher Resources on Oxford Owl. There are extra clues there as well. Try to write neatly in the middle of each square and use capital letters.

Even if you have your pen licence, use a pencil for this activity.

## Across

The name for what we do when we write letters on an angle (5 letters)

Marie Curie conducted research on this (13 letters)

Something that separates words (5 letters)

A good _____ is important when holding a pencil (4 letters)

Birth country of Louis Pasteur (6 letters)

## Down

1. Someone who creates inventions (8 letters)

2. Throughout this book I have learnt _____ handwriting (7 letters)

4. Used to take photos (6 letters)

6. Alexander Graham Bell's invention (9 letters)

7. It is important to go back over or _____ when doing horizontal joins to anti-clockwise letters. (7 letters)

# Independent writing

Write about any of the inventors or inventions that you know of or have learnt about below.
Remember to use your best cursive handwriting.